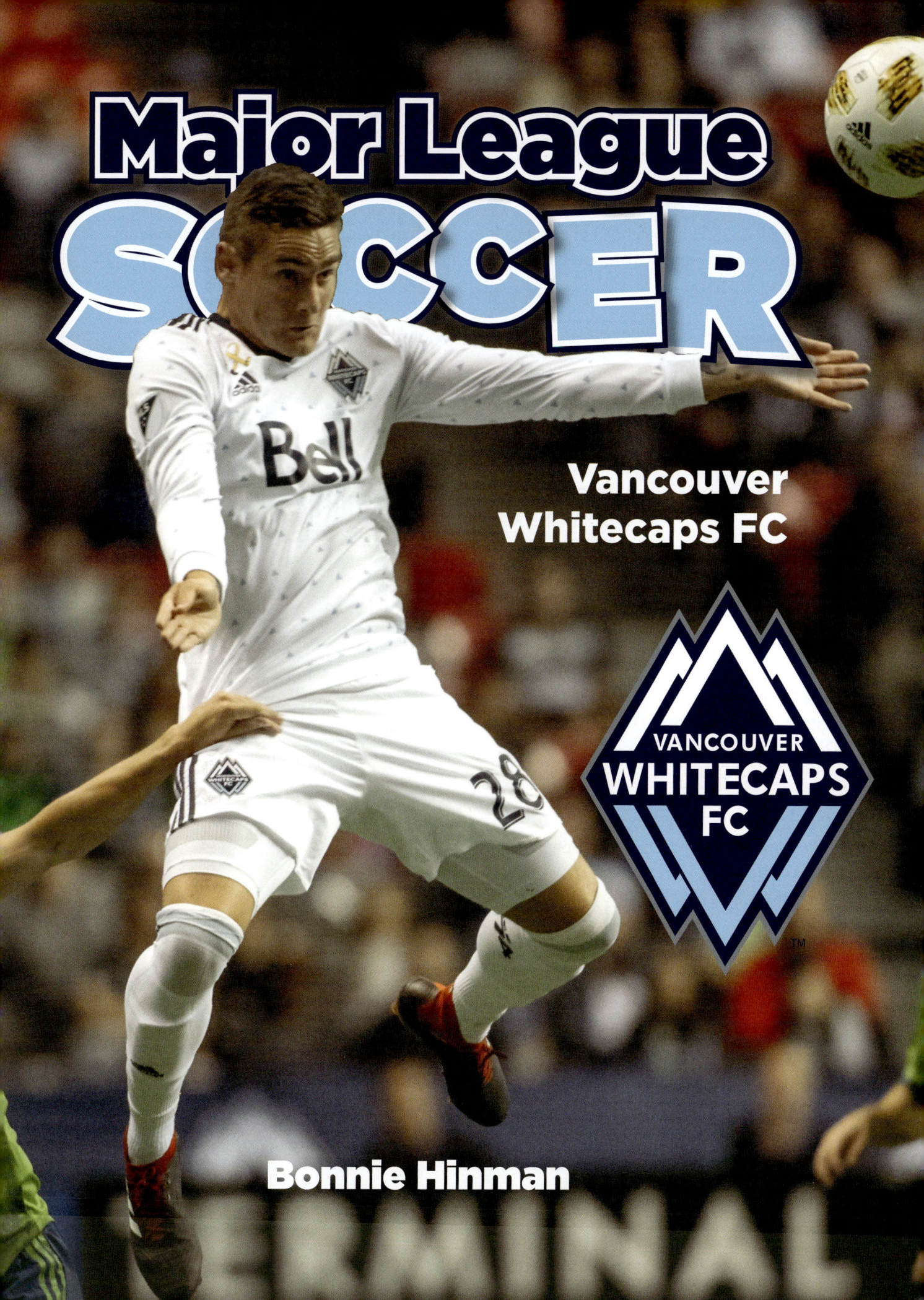

# Major League SOCCER

## Vancouver Whitecaps FC

Bonnie Hinman

Copyright © 2020 by Mitchell Lane Publishers. All rights reserved. No part of this book may be reproduced without written permission from the publisher. Printed and bound in the United States of America.

Printing     1     2     3     4     5     6     7     8

First Edition, 2020.
Author: Bonnie Hinman
Designer: Ed Morgan
Editor: Lisa Petrillo

Series: Major League Soccer
Title: Vancouver Whitecaps / by Bonnie Hinman

Hallandale, FL : Mitchell Lane Publishers, [2020]

Library bound ISBN: 9781680204940
eBook ISBN: 9781680204957

PHOTO CREDITS: Design Elements, freepik.com, Getty Images

# Contents

**Chapter One**
Major League Soccer is Born .................................................. 4

**Chapter Two**
How the Whitecaps Got Started .............................................. 8

**Chapter Three**
Let's Play Soccer ..................................................................... 14

**Chapter Four**
Whitecaps Stars ...................................................................... 18

**Chapter Five**
International Soccer Players .................................................. 24

What You Should Know ........................................................ 28
Quick Stats ............................................................................. 28
Timeline ................................................................................. 29
Glossary ................................................................................. 30
Further Reading .................................................................... 31
On the Internet ...................................................................... 31
Index ...................................................................................... 32
About the Author .................................................................. 32

Words in **bold** throughout can be found in the Glossary.

# Major League Soccer is Born

CHAPTER ONE

Soccer is the most popular sport in the world. More than 40 percent of people worldwide report that they are soccer fans. The next most popular sport is basketball at 35 percent. Soccer is called football in most other countries. It is called soccer in the U.S. and Canada. This is because the American game of football is played in those two North American countries.

Major League Soccer (MLS) officially began in April 1996. There had been other professional soccer leagues in the United States. The last one had folded in 1984. Those leagues had not been able to make enough money to survive.

In 1988 the United States was selected to host the 1994 World Cup tournament. The decision came from the Fédération Internationale de Football Association (FIFA), which in English means International Federation of Association Football. FIFA sponsors the World Cup every four years. FIFA is an international association that governs soccer clubs all over the world. Its officials provide soccer club rules. They also organize major international tournaments. The World Cup is the most famous of these tournaments.

The 2018 World Cup was held in Russia. An estimated 3.5 billion people watched on TV and in person. Thirty-two national teams played 64 matches. The French national team won the World Cup. There are often many different soccer clubs in each country. For the World Cup, the players join to make up a team from their home country. It doesn't matter where they currently play. Any soccer player can be called up to play for their country's national team.

Players from all 32 competing teams from the 2018 FIFA World Cup Russia in Russia

# Chapter One

In 1988 the United States did not have a professional soccer league. FIFA asked that the U.S. form a new professional soccer league. FIFA wanted the league started before the World Cup.

Investors and organizers began immediately to start a league. However, they were not able to get the league started before the 1994 World Cup competition was held. Major League Soccer (MLS) officially began in 1995. The first game was played April 6, 1996.

MLS began with 10 teams divided into two conferences. By 2018 there were 23 teams. There are 20 U.S. teams and 3 in Canada. They are divided into East and West conferences. Investor-operators each run their own individual teams. However, MLS is in charge rather than the individual team owners.

MLS controls the salaries of its players. The top salary allowed for a team in 2018 was $4.035 million. The 2018 maximum salary for a single player was $504,375. Most players earn much less. The 2018 minimum salary for a player was $67,500.

MLS teams do have several ways to get around the salary limits. Teams may sign a certain number of **designated** players. Called DPs, these players are allowed to be paid a higher salary. Teams use this extra money to attract star players.

Teams are also allowed to sign a certain number of homegrown players. These players must participate in a team's youth development program for at least a year. They have to live in the team's area. A homegrown player can skip the draft process. The teams sign directly with them. MLS gives teams extra money to pay homegrown players. This encourages teams to sign talented local players.

## Major League Soccer is Born

The 23 MLS teams play 34 games during the regular season March to October. They play 17 at home, and 17 away games. Teams play each of their conference (East or West) teams at least twice. All teams play each non-conference opponent one time.

MLS uses a point system to rank the teams. Each team gets three points for a win, one point for a tie, and zero points for a loss. At the end of the regular season, the team with the most points wins the Supporters' Shield Trophy.

After the regular season ends, the twelve highest ranking teams compete in a playoff series. Teams from each conference compete to win the Major League Soccer Cup.

# Fun Facts

**1** From 1919 until 1921, the first American professional soccer league, the USSA, paid its players 35 cents per goal scored.

**2** Famous Brazilian soccer player, Pelé, is the only player in the world to have been on three different World Cup winning teams.

7

# How the Whitecaps Got Started

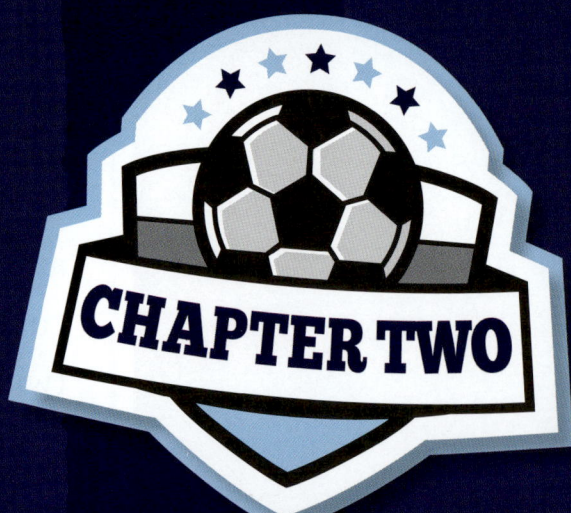

CHAPTER TWO

The Vancouver Whitecaps team played its first MLS match March 19, 2011. However, the Whitecaps existed long before that first game. On December 11, 1973, Denny Veitch and Herb Capozzi announced the start of a new soccer **franchise** based in Vancouver, British Columbia, in Southwestern Canada.

Veitch named the new team the Whitecaps. He said the name came to him one sunny day when he drove across Vancouver's Lions Gate Bridge. He looked up and saw the whitecaps on the mountains. He looked down and saw the whitecaps on the ocean. The Vancouver Whitecaps Football Club was named after the natural beauty of Vancouver.

Whitecaps play in the Soccer Bowl '79.

The team began its life playing in the North American Soccer League (NASL). The Whitecaps played in the NASL until 1984 when that league folded. In 1986 the Caps joined another new league, the Canadian Soccer League (CSL). The Whitecaps were renamed the Vancouver 86ers for that league. In 1991 the CSL also folded and the 86ers joined the American Professional Soccer League.

In 2000 the Vancouver 86ers team officially changed its name back to the Vancouver Whitecaps. The Whitecaps played in several different leagues until its first MLS game in 2011.

# Chapter Two

The Whitecaps picked navy blue, light blue, and white for their colors. Their 2018 kits or uniforms for home games were white with navy blue trim. Away or secondary kits for 2018 broke away from blue and white. They were steel gray with white trim.

BC Place in Vancouver is the current stadium for the Whitecaps. The stadium originally opened in 1983. It was remodeled in 2011. It is now a year-round open-air stadium. It has the largest **retractable** roof of its kind in the world.

The Whitecaps played the first sporting event at the original stadium in 1983. They went on to play 41 matches at the old stadium. This includes the time the team was named the 86ers.

The new MLS team played part of its first season at Empire Field. When the stadium renovation was finished, the Caps moved to BC Place. BC Place also hosts home games for the BC Lions football team. Other sporting events plus concerts and trade shows also take place at the stadium.

BC Place has seating for about 54,500 people. A canvas **drape** can be dropped over the top bowl of the seating. This reduces the seating to about 22,000. This creates a better size for soccer games.

# How the Whitecaps Got Started

Vancouver Whitecaps and Seattle Sounders stand on the field under an open roof during the national anthems prior to their match at BC Place in August 2017.

# Chapter Two

Brian Mullan (*left*) of the Colorado Rapids battles Camilo Sanvezzo of the Vancouver Whitecaps FC during their MLS game in October 2011.

From the Caps first season in 2011 through the end of the 2017 season, attendance has remained fairly steady. The total regular season home attendance in 2011 was 346,909. That total in 2017 was 364,073. With 17 home games each year, the average game attendance for the first seven years was 20,662. In 2017 that was up slightly to 21,416.

The Whitecaps have had some success as a newcomer to the MLS. In 2012 the Caps became the first Canadian team to qualify for the MLS Cup Playoffs. They have made it to the knockout round of the MLS Cup playoffs two times. They made it to the Western Conference semi-finals two times as well, in 2015 and 2017. The Caps won the Canadian Championships in 2015.

## How the Whitecaps Got Started

The Whitecaps qualified for the CONCACAF Champions League (Confederation of North, Central American and Caribbean Association Football) in the 2015-16 and 2016-17 seasons. The Champions League is an international competition. Teams from North America, Central America, and the Caribbean compete for a spot at the FIFA World Cup. The first part of the competition is played from August to December. The following year those winners play other teams from February to May. The Caps reached the Champions League semi-finals in 2016.

The Whitecaps finished the 2018 season in 8th place in the Western conference. The team did not qualify for the playoffs.

## Fun Facts

1. It takes just 20 minutes to open or close the domed roof of BC Place stadium in Vancouver.

2. In what was started as a joke, an online source claimed that soccer was illegal in Mississippi until 1991. Many readers believed the source and the story spread rapidly. Soccer has never been illegal in Mississippi.

# Let's Play Soccer

## CHAPTER THREE

For each game the Whitecaps field eleven players on the **pitch** or field. This is the rule for all MLS teams. A goalkeeper guards the team goal. Ten other players line up on the field in many different ways. Most teams arrange them in three or four lines. The coach plans the line-up as a **tactic** for winning games.

Goalkeepers must stay within an 18-yard box in front of the goal line. They are the only players who may touch the ball with their hands. They are allowed to block the ball with any part of their bodies

Defender players line up in front of the goalkeeper. Sometimes there will be four defenders. A defender's main duty is to keep the ball away from the goal line. There are several names for these defenders. They may be called right back, right center back, left back, and left center back. Sometimes they are called sweeper, full back, and wingback.

Goalkeeper (GK)
Right back defender (RB)
Left back defender (LB)
Center back defender (CB)
Left midfielder (LM)
Center midfielder (CM)
Right midfielder (RM)
Left forward (LF)
Right forward (RF)

Midfielders line up in front of the defenders on the field. There may be two, three, or even four midfielders. Midfielders often control the flow of the game. They may protect the goal with the defenders. Or they may move the ball forward toward the other goal line. Midfielders have to cover a lot of area. They have to be able to pass the ball.

Forwards line up in front of the midfielders. Sometimes they are called strikers. Their job is to get the ball over the other team's goal line. Forwards need to be fast and are often tall. But they also need to move easily down the pitch.

Like other coaches, the Caps coach decides how to line up his players. Often the Whitecaps have used a 4-2-3-1 formation of players. This means that the Caps have four forwards with two midfielders right behind them. Three defenders line up in front of the goalkeeper. Sometimes the Caps use a 4-1-4-1 formation.

# Chapter Three

Actress Georgina Haig with the Whitecap's mascot Spike during the Legends & Stars: Whitecaps FC charity alumni match at BC Place in September 2017

Spike is the Vancouver Whitecaps' team **mascot**. Spike is a belted kingfisher. Kingfishers are birds that live in the Vancouver area. Whitecaps officials like to joke that Spike is tall for a bird, and likes to eat fish tacos. Spike took over for Winger, the team's former mascot who retired in 2011.

The Whitecaps' biggest **rivals** are the Seattle Sounders and the Portland Timbers. The teams were strong rivals long before any of them were in the MLS. Each team has strong supporters. They are located in the Pacific Northwest.

Each year since 2004 the three rival teams compete against each other to win the Cascadia Cup trophy. The competition awards the trophy to the best soccer team in the Pacific Northwest. The Caps won the Cascadia Cup 6 times. The most recent Cup win was in 2016.

# Let's Play Soccer

The Whitecaps are known for using cross passes. A cross is a pass that often comes from near the edge of the field. The ball is directed toward the area in front of the goal. A cross is intended to be headed or kicked into the goal by a teammate.

Head coach of the Whitecaps, Carl Robinson, was fired in September 2018 with just five games left in the season. Robinson had been head coach since December 2013. Although Robinson's record as coach was decent, the team's 2018 season was **turbulent**. Robinson and the team officials argued about contracts for his coaching staff.

After two key losses in September to Dallas and Seattle, Whitecaps owners fired Robinson on September 25, 2018. **Professional** soccer observers said that the Whitecaps were too **inconsistent** in 2018. In professional sports, winning games is considered the most important measure of a team's success. The Whitecaps did not win enough games in 2018. The team finished the 2018 season in 8th place in the Western Conference. The Caps did not qualify for the playoffs.

# Fun Facts

1. Australia set a world record for the largest victory in an international match. On April 11, 2001, Australia defeated American Samoa 31-0.

2. The Adidas Futsal Park is located on the roof of a department store in Tokyo, Japan. Futsal is a soccer-like sport that is played on a smaller pitch. Futsal teams play with five players on each side.

# Whitecaps Stars

## CHAPTER FOUR

Brazilian Camilo Sanvezzo was the first star of the Whitecaps. He signed with the club in March 2011. This was just before the team's first game in the MLS. The striker scored 12 goals in that first season. This was the most goals of anyone on the team. Sanvezzo was named Whitecaps FC Player of the Year for 2011.

Sanvezzo began his career in the youth programs in Brazil. He went on to play in Malta and South Korea. His impressive tryout with the Whitecaps led to his signing with Vancouver.

The year 2013 was a great one for Sanvezzo. He was the high scorer in all of MLS. He scored 22 goals that season. Rumors soon began that he would transfer to a different club.

Sanvezzo moved to the Mexican club Querétaro FC in January 2014. The Querétaro club paid a multimillion-dollar transfer fee. Camilo still plays for Querétaro.

Camilo Sanvezzo at the 2012 Amway Canadian Championship against the Toronto FC in May 2012

# Chapter Four

Kei Kamara has been called the best Whitecaps forward since Camilo Sanvezzo. Kamara is a newcomer to the Whitecaps. He was traded to the team in December 2017. Kamara was born and grew up in Sierra Leone, Africa. His family came to the United States as **refugees** when he was 16. He became an American citizen in 2006.

Kamara began his MLS career in 2006. He played for Columbus Crew. He later played for several other MLS teams. He was also loaned to the English Premier League at Norwich. He came to the Whitecaps from the New England Revolution club.

Kamara was a MLS All-Star in 2015. He won the MLS Works **Humanitarian** of the Year Award in 2015. He was also the MLS Cup Playoffs top-scorer in 2015. In 2018 Kamara became one of only ten MLS players in history to score 100 goals in their careers.

In the 2018 season Kamara was the highest scorer for the Whitecaps. He scored 14 goals with 6 assists. That was almost twice as many goals as any other Whitecaps player. He played in 28 games for a total of 2,167 minutes, demonstrating his athletic ability and training.

# Whitecaps Stars

Kei Kamara (*top*) heads the ball over Leonardo of Houston Dynamo at BC Place in May 2018.

# Chapter Four

Alphonso Davies waves to the crowd after his last game with the Whitecaps in October 2018.

Whitecaps midfielder Alphonso Davies is a homegrown player for the club. Davies was born in a refugee camp on November 2, 2000, in Ghana, Africa. His parents **emigrated** to Canada. He grew up in Edmonton, Canada, and played youth soccer there. Davies joined the Whitecaps FC Residency program in August 2015 at the age of 14.

Davies is the star of the Whitecaps youth development program. He progressed quickly through the age levels. He moved to the Whitecaps second team when he was 15. In July 2016 he signed a contract with the Whitecaps first team—when he was still only age 15. He was the youngest active player in MLS.

# Whitecaps Stars

Davies gained his Canadian citizenship in June 2017. A week later he joined the Canadian national team. At age 16, Davies was the first player born in the 21st century to score at a major international tournament.

In 2017 Davies won the CONCACAF Gold Cup Golden Boot Award. In 2018 he was named a MLS All-Star. In July 2018 the Whitecaps signed a transfer deal. Davies was heading to the German team FC Bayern Munich. The agreement included a record-breaking transfer fee. The Whitecaps will receive $13.5 million from Bayern. Additional bonuses could raise the amount to $22 million. This is a record for MLS.

Davies ended his career with the Whitecaps with a bang. In the very last game of the season on October 28, 2018, he scored two goals. At the end of an up and down season, the Whitecaps players celebrated with their young teammate. His next playing time would be in Germany.

# Fun Facts

1. Attending the World Cup Final is expensive for fans. The best seats at the 2018 World Cup Final in Russia went for $1,100. Tickets were resold for as much as $2,500.

2. The biggest soccer stadium in the world is Rungrado May Day Stadium in Pyongyang, North Korea. It can seat around 150,000 fans.

# International Soccer Players

## CHAPTER FIVE

Major League Soccer likes to attract players from other countries. Soccer players face stiff competition in Europe and South America. Those teams have been active for decades. They have dedicated fans and take in plenty of money. They can afford to hire the best players in the world.

In 2018, MLS allowed 184 international player spots. These are divided among the 23 teams, at 8 for each team. Teams may trade these spots. Some teams have more than 8 international players while others have fewer than 8. Teams may also loan players to each other. There is no limit to how many international players a team can have. However, the spots must be gained by trading or loaning between teams.

In 2018, Major League Soccer had 184 international players out of 660 total players. These international players come to the U.S. for many different reasons. Some players in the United States were stars in Europe but got cut for one reason or another. Some sign for a chance to come to the United States.

Life can be hard for international players new to the United States. They may not speak English. During games this often doesn't matter. Soccer has a language of its own. New players learn a few words in English such as offside, foul, and goal. Referees use whistles, signals, and hand signs to talk to players. Every soccer player understands the yellow and red card system for foul penalties.

# Chapter Five

Some soccer words are even the same in different languages. Foul is *fallo* in Italian. Pass is *passe* in Portuguese and *pase* in Spanish. There are other words that sound similar in different languages.

Life for an international player off the pitch is more complicated. MLS players travel much more and farther than players in other countries. The large size of the United States makes this necessary. Many players in Europe or South America travel only a few hours by train or bus to play away games. There are limited times that MLS players can avoid traveling by airplane. These increased travel demands are hard on new international players.

Playing conditions on the fields also vary widely. A team might play one night in Vancouver where it is 75 degrees and misty. Overnight teammembers might fly to Houston to play a game in 105-degree Fahrenheit temperatures. A former European player might be fine in Vancouver but wilt in the heat and humidity of Houston. The opposite might be true of a former South American player.

Cultural differences between the United States and an international player's home country can be startling. The food is different, and so is the money. A player may

# International Soccer Players

have lived in a small house in a small town before coming to the U.S. Now he may live in a huge apartment building in a big city.

One of the adjustments that can be hard for some international players is the style of the game. MLS is a high-speed league. Players attack quickly. The play can seem chaotic. European leagues in particular often use a slower, more thoughtful style. Even the best international players can be confused. One style is not better than another. They are just different.

Some international players adjust quickly to all the changes. Others never do and are gone in a season. Vancouver and other teams try to choose international players who will adjust. But it's always hard to tell until the player is here and playing. All players, including international ones, have to want to play. They have to focus on playing soccer rather than the off-field problems. International players just have a few more off-field problems to deal with.

# Fun Facts

1. **The World Cup trophy stands 14.4 inches (36.5 centimeters) tall and weighs 13.61 pounds (6.175 kg). It was worth approximately $161,000 in 2018.**

2. **Soccer was the first team sport added to the Olympic Games. It was added to the games as a regular competition in 1908.**

# What You Should Know

- Soccer is called football in most countries.
- More than 40 percent of adults worldwide say they are soccer fans.
- The first Major League Soccer game was played on April 6, 1996.
- The Soccer World Cup Tournament is held every four years.
- In 2018 the World Cup Finals were held in Russia.
- The Vancouver Whitecaps first played in 1974 in the North American Soccer League.
- The Whitecaps were called the Vancouver 86ers from 1986 to 1999.
- The Vancouver 86ers changed their name back to the Whitecaps in 2000.
- The Vancouver Whitecaps joined MLS in 2011.
- Vancouver is one of three Canadian teams in the MLS.
- The Whitecaps play at BC Place stadium.
- In 2012 the Whitecaps became the first Canadian team to qualify for the MLS Cup playoffs.

## Quick Stats

| | |
|---|---|
| Total regular season games played | 272 |
| Total games won | 96 |
| Total games lost | 104 |
| Total games a tie | 72 |
| Total goals scored | 359 |
| Total goals scored against Vancouver | 385 |
| Total points earned | 360 |

# Vancouver Timeline

**1973**     A new soccer franchise is announced in Vancouver, Canada.

**1974**     The original Vancouver Whitecaps play their first game in the NASL.

**1986**     The Whitecaps are renamed the Vancouver 86ers.

**1995**     Major League Soccer is established in the U.S.

**2011**     Whitecaps play their first game in the MLS.

**2012**     Whitecaps become the first Canadian team to qualify for the MLS Cup Playoffs.

**2015**     Whitecaps win the Canadian Championships.

**2018**     Whitecaps sign multi-million dollar transfer deal for star Alphonso Davies in July.

**2018**     Whitecaps coach Carl Robinson is fired in September.

**2018**     Whitecaps finish in eighth place in the Western Conference.

# Glossary

**designated**  To choose for a particular job or position

**drape**  To cover or hang with cloth

**franchise**  The right or license given to a company or group to operate in a specific territory

**humanitarian**  Doing something for the good of others

**emigrated**  To leave your home country and move to another

**inconsistent**  Two or more actions or elements that do not agree or remain the same

**mascot**  An animal, person, or thing that is considered to bring good luck

**pitch**  The name for a soccer playing field

**professional**  Doing a job as a way of making money

**refugee**  A person who flees his or her country to find safety elsewhere

**retractable**  Something that can be pulled back

**rival**  A team that another team wants to defeat

**tactic**  A plan for getting a desired outcome such as winning a soccer game

**turbulent**  Being disturbed and changing often

## Further Reading

Folger, Carlos and Crisfield, Deborah W. *The Everything Kids' Soccer Book, 4th Edition: Rules, Techniques, and More about Your Favorite Sport!* New York: Simon and Schuster, 2018.

Latham, Andrew. *Soccer smarts for Kids: 60 Skills, Strategies, and Secrets.* Berkeley, CA: Rockridge Press, 2016.

Simon, Eddy. *Pele: The King of Soccer.* New York: First Second Books, 2017.

## On the Internet

**The Best FIFA Men's Player, 2018**
https://www.fifa.com/the-best-fifa-football-awards/best-fifa-mens-player/

**FIFA World Cup 2022 Stadiums**
http://www.stadiumguide.com/tournaments/fifa-world-cup-2022-stadiums-qatar/

**Spotlight on Alphonso Davies**
https://www.mlssoccer.com/post/2018/10/05/caps-phenom-davies-real-deal-youth-spotlight-pres-target?autoplay=true

## Index

| | |
|---|---|
| BC Place | 10, 16, 21 |
| Davies, Alphonso | 22, 23 |
| FIFA (Federation Internationale de Football Association) | 5, 6, 13 |
| Kamara, Kei | 20, 21 |
| MLS (Major League Soccer) | 4, 6, 16, 18 |
| All Stars | 20, 22, 23 |
|   and Whitecaps | 8, 9 |
|   Cup | 7, 12 |
|   conferences | 6, 12 |
|   international players | 24, 25, 26, 27 |
| Robinson, Carl | 17 |
| Sanvezzo, Camilo | 12, 18, 19, |
| Whitecaps | 8, 11, 13, 14, 15, 17 |
|   attendance | 12 |
|   colors | 10 |
|   mascot | 16 |
|   star players | 18, 19, 20, 22, 23 |
| World Cup Tournament | 5, 6, 7, 13, 23, 27 |

## About the Author

**Bonnie Hinman** began following MLS clubs after writing about the Vancouver Whitecaps FC and other exciting teams. She loves to learn more about a professional sport. Hinman has written more than 50 books, most of them nonfiction. She lives in Southwest Missouri with her husband Bill near her children and five grandchildren.